Evangelism:
The Process

Jeffrey Battles

TRILOGY CHRISTIAN PUBLISHERS
Tustin, CA

Trilogy Christian Publishers
A Wholly Owned Subsidiary of Trinity Broadcasting Network
2442 Michelle Drive
Tustin, CA 92780

Evangelism: The Process

Copyright © 2022 by Jeffrey Battles

Scripture quotations marked NLT are taken from the Holy Bible, New Living Translation, copyright © 1996, 2004, 2015 by Tyndale House Foundation. Used by permission of Tyndale House Publishers, Inc., Carol Stream, Illinois 60188. All rights reserved. Scripture quotations marked KJV are taken from the King James Version of the Bible. Public domain.

No part of this book may be reproduced, stored in a retrieval system, or transmitted by any means without written permission from the author. All rights reserved. Printed in the USA.

Rights Department, 2442 Michelle Drive, Tustin, CA 92780.

Trilogy Christian Publishing/TBN and colophon are trademarks of Trinity Broadcasting Network.

Cover design by: __

For information about special discounts for bulk purchases, please contact Trilogy Christian Publishing.

Trilogy Disclaimer: The views and content expressed in this book are those of the author and may not necessarily reflect the views and doctrine of Trilogy Christian Publishing or the Trinity Broadcasting Network.

Manufactured in the United States of America

10 9 8 7 6 5 4 3 2 1

Library of Congress Cataloging-in-Publication Data is available.

ISBN: 978-1-68556-915-0

E-ISBN: 978-1-68556-916-7 (ebook)

Dedication

I want to dedicate this book to, first and foremost, my family. There are so many who volunteer to be on the stage once there is one, but very few want to participate in the "process." My wife and children have stood strong from the very beginning. It wasn't easy. To have to say goodbye so many times as I would board a plane to be gone for weeks, my wife had to take on our home at times on her own. She'd receive phone calls of me being sick and hospitalized in a third-world country, getting calls about me potentially getting arrested if we held the crusade. She often had greater burdens as my wife than even myself being in the field.

Two-point six million souls led to Christ to the date of this book being published are directly connected to the backbone of this ministry, my wife and kids. I also want to dedicate this book to every man or woman with a fire for the lost. For every person who is willing to give up their own plans for the sake of the gospel, I respect you and honor you. It doesn't take a special person to be an evangelist on fire; it takes a dead person—a person who has died to themselves and lives for Jesus. The sacrifices you will make, most will never see. They may never know. I want you to know that I understand. I am with you and will be praying for you to endure until the end. I pray for your family. I pray for a hedge of protection around you physically, emotionally, and spiritually—the greater your commitment, the greater the anointing, and the greater the works. The content of this book is to prepare you for and walk you through one of the most challenging yet rewarding roads you will ever take in this short span of time on this earth. Many are called, but few are chosen. There is a harvest attached to your obedience. This is the beginning for many of you. Embrace the process that most give up on. The process is where your story is written.

Contents

Chapter 1. Have No Idea Where to Start 1

Chapter 2. He Knows You Aren't Ready, Nobody Is 7

Chapter 3. Salvation, Still the Hardest Miracle to Accept 16

Chapter 4. It Will Only Cost You Everything 22

Chapter 5. It's Time 36

CHAPTER 1

I Have No Idea Where to Start

Some of you will begin to read this book and disqualify yourself as an evangelist simply because of what has been said about you, what you have done, or even what you have not done. I have good news for you: nothing you can do can qualify you. Without Jesus, not one of us is qualified. But with Jesus, the chains begin to fall off. When you understand that our righteousness is like filthy rags, you will stop rating your own performance as a means of qualification. I have preached to millions of people over the last few years, and to this day, the weight of who I used to be still wears me out at times. I have even had pastors call other pastors to tell them about "my past." I remember coming home from a mission in the Middle East, and I would be on fire after tens of thousands of souls came to Jesus, but I would have to stay quiet about it at my home church because of the self-righteous judgment from those who knew who I was years before. At first, nobody knew what was happening but eventually, the word started to spread, and I was given about one to two minutes behind the pulpit to fit in all the miracles and salvation that took place during the mission. The congregation was hungry for more, but the leadership was full before I even took a step toward the pulpit. When I was swimming in sin, I was welcome, but when I had an encounter with Jesus and my little spark turned into a forest fire, I became the talk of the church behind closed doors. Almost as if I was breaking a church code by going to places to preach that I didn't see anyone else going to. Most outreaches I would see were within a few miles of the church, where the church could benefit from the harvest with another seat being filled and another tither. Local outreach is so important, but the intentions must be pure. The greatest benefit to local outreach is local discipleship! I wanted to reach the ones who couldn't pay. I didn't have an overhead; I didn't have a building to pay for, so I thought, *Why not invest in souls and bring the church out to them?* I have always believed that if the church doesn't send, it will eventually end. It is time we invest into the body what we have invested into the temple.

    I will admit, after hearing it from people I was supposed to be learning from, I started to second guess myself. Questioning if what I had done in my past was really more powerful than the blood. Was my purpose to warm a pew and fill the plate as it passed three times a week? Then I began to realize God was never bringing up my past, just my pastor. I remember coming back from a crusade in Africa, and a woman was healed on the spot of cancer. She even brought her doctor's report months later just to prove what she already knew. I was in prayer and fasting for God to take away my anger toward my old church. I would hear of failure after failure happening there after I left, and secretly and sometimes openly, I would rejoice at their repayment for how they treated my family and me, who served in three different ministries there. This was when God spoke directly to me. He said, "Jeff, I will give you what you want, but you have to choose. I won't give you both. When you lay your hands on the sick who come for miles to hear you preach My Word, I will be with you, and the sick will be healed. Or I will give you revenge. Whichever occupies your heart the most, I will grant you." I began to weep. I recalled the woman who was healed crying saying to me that she could not believe God did this for her. I knew an evangelist without the anointing of the Holy Ghost is simply a motivational speaker referencing the Bible. Daily repentance is key to remaining humble to where Christ gets the glory for everything.

Most evangelists do not know the Bible front to back, not like a scholar or even a doctor of theology. When I first started out, I had two or three sermons that I would get fired up on every time I would preach them. I have learned that a pastor preaches a different message to the same crowd, but an evangelist preaches the same message to a different crowd. Both are extremely important in the kingdom of God. I remember telling a man who had recently given his heart to Christ and was asking me how to go about becoming an evangelist. He said he only knew a couple of scriptures by heart. I said, "Brother, if all you know is John 3:16, then you preach John 3:16 and attach it to your testimony of how Jesus saved you. Your love for the gospel will grow, and you will dig more into the Word and will eventually preach heaven down to earth. It is better to believe the one scripture you know than to know a hundred sermons, but the moment a crisis hits, you prove you didn't believe even one of the sermons. Do not wait for a platform to come to you. Go make one. Preach to anyone who will listen, even if that one is yourself. Volunteer at your local church. Understand what it means to serve. Your first message will be how you treat others, especially when they have messed up." I believe the majority of American Christians could go to Northern Nigeria or Afghanistan, where Christians are persecuted, and be perfectly safe. They only persecute Christians who do the will of the Father. Evangelist, you are the one who will carry the fire of Jesus to the streets in your church. Jesus never once said to bring the sinners to the church;

He said to bring the church to the sinners. This is your duty, your purpose. You will develop a burning desire for souls. When I am about thirty days in between missions and have not done an altar call for a period of time, I get weak and feel dead. Seeing hands go in the air for salvation brings renewal to my life every time. In fact, through the hundreds of altar calls I have done, I fight back the tears each and every time. I usually lose the battle. I remember being lost like it was yesterday, and I remember what it felt like to realize how much God loved me for the first time. Bring that gift to the world. Your obedience to the call over your life unlocks an anointing that you will never want to live without. I would encourage you to preach your first sermons to your own house. They may not listen to you because they know who you are, but they will see you. They will see you begin to live for Jesus. This is the sermon that they will receive better than the one you speak. Nobody can deny a tree full of fruit. They may not like it, but they will see it. Concern yourself with the souls in your home before anything else. We are not responsible for the outcome, but we are responsible for the delivery. Include your family as often as you can. Your spouse will cover your blind spots for you. They will see things coming that you cannot.

Why did I include so much of what happened to me at my local church? To prepare you. A wolf always hides in sheep's clothing. The devil will not use a critic you do not know to take you out. He will send someone close to you who knows how to hurt you. Matthew 10:16 (NLT) says, "Look, I am sending you out as sheep among wolves. So be as shrewd as snakes and harmless as doves." The devil doesn't just want you to be hurt; he wants you to quit. I mentioned that I had no issues at church when I was in sin and sitting in the pew, but when I started winning souls, it began ... The devil doesn't care if you go to church as long as you don't start becoming the church. The time is now. When Jesus said, "Follow Me," the disciples began saying to Him that they needed to go see their families first, and Jesus said, "There is no time for that." There is no time to look back. The last person to look back was Lot's wife. God knows you are not fully ready; that is His job, not yours; you just have to choose to "go." You do what you can, and the Spirit of God will do what you cannot. There will always be someone who knows more than you, speaks better than you, and has more charisma than you. If you always compare yourself to someone more qualified than you but less willing, you will usually suffer from analysis paralysis. Stop comparing your weakness to someone else's strength. You may only have one strong point and a hundred weak points. That one strong point may be the very detail that God is going to use in that season. Trust Him. If He can form everything in six days by just speaking it into existence, He knows how and when to do it with you.

CHAPTER 2

He Knows You Aren't Ready, Nobody Is

Matthew 16:18 (KJV) says, "And I say also unto thee, That thou art Peter, and upon this rock I will build my church; and the gates of hell shall not prevail against it." What an extremely bold statement from Jesus to Peter, considering the choices Peter was about to make in the near future. This conversation was spoken in Caesarea Philippi, the very location they believed to be the entrance to hell at that time. Jesus was giving Peter a revelation. In Matthew 26, Jesus began to tell the disciples that one of them would desert Him and deny Him. Of course, Peter declared that even if everyone else deserted Jesus, he would be the last man standing. Jesus began to explain to Peter that he would be the one that would do it. Peter got angry, saying, "I will even die with You, Jesus!" Now, this was a very bold statement from Peter.

I believe he said that believing 100 percent this would be the case. The definition of commitment is "simply doing what you say you will do even when the mood you say it in leaves you." Clearly, the environment where this proclamation was said was not hostile, and the disciples had not experienced the environment but merely listened to Jesus' claim of what was coming. Oftentimes as evangelists or wanting to become evangelists, we see a Billy Graham crusade or a Bonnke crusade, and we see the result but rarely do we see the process. Everyone wants to be an evangelist at the crusade, but when it comes to the planning, the money it takes, the betrayal you face, etc., some will begin to question how far and how big they really want to go! It is easy to commit from a church pew, but the mission field brings a new reality.

Not long after Peter claimed he would never leave Jesus, they proceeded to the Garden of Gethsemane. Jesus took a few steps past as He told His disciples to keep watch while He went on to pray. The scripture says Jesus was anguished to the point of death. As Jesus walked back and found the disciples sleeping, He did not address them all by name but only one of them, "Peter, why can you not stay awake for just one hour!" Leaders are held to a higher standard, especially when greatness is expected of them. Three times Jesus came back and found them sleeping. Not long after, they went to arrest Jesus. Peter aggressively attacked the soldier with a sword and cut off his ear. Jesus quickly placed the ear back on the soldier and healed him. Jesus did not do this because He felt bad for the soldier. The following morning after Jesus' arrest, Peter was spotted and accused of being with Jesus. This was when he began to deny it. Jesus knew that if Peter had cut the ear off that soldier that next morning, they wouldn't have questioned him; they would have killed him. Jesus saw past Peter's mistakes and saw his potential. Jesus patched up Peter's mistake when He fixed the soldier's ear. Somewhat of a prophecy of what Jesus was about to do for the whole world.

In Mark 16:15, Jesus called the disciples to the Great Commission, telling them to go tell the whole world that they need to repent and the kingdom of heaven is near. But, in 16:11, the Bible says they were in unbelief. In 16:13, they were in unbelief. In 16:14, Jesus rebuked them for their unbelief. But 16:15, He commissioned them to go forth. In this entire conversation, Jesus was talking to men who were full of unbelief. Oftentimes we see the most unqualified people in man's eyes doing some of the greatest works for the Lord. This is why the largest evangelistic moves were non-denominational or organized-church sponsored. Oftentimes the ones God uses would be benched by the elders.

In 2015, my family had left, and I was in my home alone. I spent at least thirty days without leaving my home, crying, praying, and repenting. It was a fast of almost twenty days. It was the middle of the night. I woke up and had a pistol next to my bed. I was at my end, and I knew this was it for me. I grabbed the pistol, and at that very moment, I heard talking downstairs in my home. My home was supposed to be empty, so I walked down the steps with my gun. The sound was coming from my office. So I walked into the office and realized that my computer was playing a sermon, a sermon I never put on the computer. In fact, the computer wasn't even on. I literally had to turn the computer on before I could turn it off. I went back to bed. And I realized as Psalm 77:6 says, "I call to remembrance my song in the night: I meditate within my heart, and my spirit makes diligent search." It was the first time I could say that God did the supernatural to reveal Himself to me. Interestingly enough, the first radio program Billy Graham took over was called *Songs in the Night*. He came at my darkest hour when I came to the end of my strength. He spoke to me through a computer that was not even on. There was no other man in that room that night; therefore, no other man could ordain or qualify me to win the lost. It was a couple of days later, as I was lying on my floor, could barely move from about twenty days of no food, that I heard a voice. This voice spoke, "Hey, My son. I have a job for you." (I thought to myself, *After all the preaching I have ever heard, I will never do a thing in the church again.*) God said, "You are right. I am not calling you into the church; I am calling you to be the church to the world." It brought a whole new meaning to me of when Jesus was calling the unbelieving disciples. He does not call the qualified; He qualifies the called. I remember the first time I was approached by someone talking about the places I go to preach. He said, "Jeff, do you realize that you could be jailed or even killed in some of these places?" I remember laughing and telling him, "Well, I have been in jail before, and I attempted to kill myself three different times. If I can't kill myself, I am betting the enemy will have a hard time with it too." Of course, he laughed, but the very things in my life that the religious said were why I would never be able to serve are the things God used to send me to the places where the religious would never go. Not a day goes by that I do not dread who I was. It follows me everywhere. It keeps the glory from going to Jesus. In my own strength, I am nothing. I was never good enough. But Jesus is.

I recall that in the very beginning, I was given advice from a thirty-year veteran as an evangelist. I had made up my mind that I was going to listen to the advice I agreed with, but what I didn't, I would disregard. Three years later, I had to return to my evangelist friend and laugh and tell him that he was right.

I was sold on preaching salvation, but I was not sold on preaching on the healing power of the Holy Spirit.

Why? Because I would have to demonstrate it. There is no possible way God would ever trust me with the miraculous. In fact, on every mission I was on and returned to my home country, I was reminded of how I was completely out of order for just going without the support of a local church. I remember my first gospel crusade in the Middle East. I was in the middle of the sermon, and two Muslim women brought a lifeless child to the altar. I completely froze. All I could think about was the woman with the issue of blood, and I could not have security remove them. I remember kneeling over this little boy. I just started weeping. All I could do was repent before God. I remember crying out to God, saying if I had known that He would use me like this, I never would have chosen the paths I had chosen. My tears reached the little boy. I stood up and finished my sermon. The women removed the lifeless body in sorrow. The altar call was incredible that night. Approximately 85 percent of the crowd raised their hands to receive salvation. I should have been celebrating, but I still felt a little empty.

EVANGELISM: THE PROCESS

It was one year after that mission when I was approached by the pastors who were at that very crusade. They said, "Pastor Jeff, do you remember that little boy at the crusade last year?" I said, "Of course I do." I felt the embarrassment rising up. "He fully recovered and is with his mom, and everything is fine," they said. Somewhere between the mother and son's journey from the stage to their home, Jesus woke him up. I made them show me a photo for proof. Even I didn't believe it. I realized something, Jesus was going to heal at these meetings whether I was ready or not. He reminded me that His hand does not move based on how good or bad I have been. His hand moves because He is good all the time. I learned a valuable lesson on that trip. He is in charge, not me. That very same mission, we were ministering in a village off the beaten path. A seven-year-old girl came for prayer with a tumor on her neck. We prayed over her. I remember getting a little broken in my emotions, reminding God she had nothing. She had no opportunity to go to the doctor first, medicine next, and so on. This was the only shot she had: God's healing or nothing. It didn't feel very promising after prayer. Sometimes the constant thought of who we used to be creates a mental block of hindrance. As I was walking out of the home, I felt a boldness overcome me and a strength of promise. I turned around and said to her, "The next time I see you, you will be completely healed." I walked out of there believing that on my next trip to Pakistan, when I found her, I would get the report of the Lord.

It was about twenty-four hours later I was preaching to a crowd of about 500. I saw a little girl in the crowd who resembled the same girl from the day before. We called her to the front and asked if she was the little one we prayed for. She pointed at her neck and put her hands up, saying, "The tumor disappeared!" I picked her up in my arms in front of the crowd and gave her the microphone. She testified as to what the Lord had done for her. Almost everyone at the meeting repented and surrendered to God that night. I will never forget that night. I will never forget that little face and her smile. I was surprised, but she wasn't. She did not come for prayer in hopes of a miracle. She came expecting a miracle. I might not have been ready, but Jesus was. It wasn't me who had to perform the miracle; I just had to be the conduit for the Spirit of God to work through. You cannot unsee a miracle. The true miracle wasn't the tumor disappearing; it was the 500 people who believed and were saved. He knows you aren't ready, but He is!

CHAPTER 3

Salvation, Still the Hardest Miracle to Accept

Luke 7:39 (NLT) says, "If this man were a prophet, he would know what kind of woman is touching him. She's a sinner!" Acts 9:13 (NLT) says, "'But Lord,' exclaimed Ananias, 'I've heard many people talk about the terrible things this man has done to the believers in Jerusalem!'" Acts 28:4 (NLT) says, "The people of the island saw the viper hanging from his hand and said to each other, 'A murderer, no doubt! Though he escaped the sea, justice will not permit him to live!'" Over and over again, we read that people, including the church, have an idea of who is qualified and who is not. Over the years, I have seen cheering and shouting if blind eyes open, if tumors disappear, or if money comes out of nowhere when the need is greater than the supply. I have seen pulpits occupied with thirty-second testimonials of a need that was met. If we just give a little more in the offering, He will do it for us too. In Luke Chapter 7, Jesus was in Simon's house filled with other Pharisees. When Mary came in and started anointing Jesus, they started bringing up her past to tell Jesus that she was garbage, that she was a horrible person, and that she shouldn't even be touching Him. In all reality, they were only upset that Jesus was paying attention to her and not them. When Jesus went to the cross, all the men who watched Him walk on water and perform miracles were gone. But at the tomb to seek out Jesus' body was a woman named Mary Magdalene. Jesus told her to go tell the disciples that He had risen. Now many can die on the cross, but only one has ever risen Himself from the dead. The message she was told to deliver has been preached on Resurrection Sunday for over 2000 years, "He has risen." The woman Jesus told to go deliver this message was the same woman being shamed by the religious at Simon's table. The religious saw her past; Jesus saw she would be the only one left at the tomb. Not much has changed today. God has been a "watch this" kind of God since the beginning. Every time the experts of rules set the guidelines for God, He's shown them He is still in charge. In Acts Chapter 9, Ananias was told to go lay hands on Saul of Tarsus. He pleaded with Jesus, making sure Jesus knew the past of Saul. Obviously, letting Jesus know He was making a mistake. Clearly, there are people outside of the temple who pray wonderful prayers using eloquent words, who have never been caught in sin, and whom Jesus should be calling on. Jesus' reply was pretty simple. Essentially He said to go and do what He told him. Jesus said, "Ananias, you have no idea how much this man will suffer for My name's sake." Jesus never spoke about blessings that he would receive or healing miracles; He said: "suffer." Your calling will not always have a cherry on top. In fact, it will come with great suffering and persecution. It will cost many of you close friendships; even family will abandon your vision. Some of you will get run down, put down, and turned down. The fulfillment of your call is not based on feelings, emotions, or the approval of others. From the moment the scale fell from Saul's eyes, he went to work. He had the approval of nobody but Jesus. The apostle Paul never forgot who he was and where he came from. In fact, it came up in most of his messages. Almost everywhere he went, if it was not fresh in his mind from his own thoughts, someone else was there to bring it up. Paul performed more miracles than anyone else in the New Testament besides Jesus. I have realized that the only way to avoid criticism is to avoid your calling. Paul got less criticism than Saul. Mary only got ridiculed when Jesus gave her attention. This has not changed in 2000 years. If you bring any physical miracle to the religious, they will cheer, especially if it is a member of their ministry. But when you tell them a former drug addict is winning souls in the streets or that a former prostitute is bringing girls off the streets into the house of God, they think there is no way someone who made a mistake in the public eye is fit for ministry. They must sit under a man who never got caught! The five-fold ministry has been reduced to three-fold—me, myself, and I. Every calling is different for each individual person. We must leave room. Jesus specializes in "watch this" moments. He has a way of using the unusable and transforming them from the inside out. He uses people who were so far gone so that there is no way that man can get the glory. This is not to boast about past sinful living; it is simply to prove that His blood is greater than our sin.

I was only home from a mission for a couple of days and visited a local church with a pastor I know very well. He came up to me privately and said, "I cannot say this publicly," but privately, he said he was very proud of me and was amazed at what God was doing with our ministry team and me. Most would take it as a compliment, but for me, I heard, "Hey Jeff, some still do not believe after all these years you are changed, and mentioning you or your ministry would cause problems." This was in the month of December. Just under 700,000 souls came to Christ that year through Impact Nations Global. I was qualified to work in three different ministries and had keys to the church until I was called to the mission field. The greatest persecution has never come from the world but from other Christians. The great news is the calling comes from God, the anointing comes from God, salvation comes from God, and the approval comes from God. No matter how many men speak against you, the opinions of sheep should never supersede the call of a lion. The only way to avoid criticism is to avoid your purpose. Paul said in Acts that his life was meaningless unless he was fulfilling the purpose he had in Christ. Paul's persecutors are gone, but Paul's messages are still here. Our lives are meaningless outside the purpose we have in Jesus Christ. The enemy will use anyone, including those close to you or those you respect, to get you to quit. I have realized over the years that the millions of souls who have given their hearts to Christ did not care about who I was in my past but were more concerned about who Jesus is. The people who are concerned about who I was in the past are not my assignment. As an evangelist, your purpose is to win the lost, not justify yourself to the already saved. I have learned that a tree among other trees doesn't stand out. But a tree with fruit among trees that only have leaves will always be the first tree they try to cut down. Surround yourself in the vineyard with other trees with fruit. They need light and nourishment just like you to remain fruitful. They have the same purpose and the same process to remain fruitful. Remember cutting down dead trees is not your job. All dead branches will be cut by the owner of the forest. Our job is to plant new trees. Salvation and the change that comes from salvation are not done by any evangelist or pastor but by the powerful work of the Holy Spirit. Of all of the doubts and criticism, I give God the glory. It is a constant reminder that I need to die daily. Do not give satisfaction to anyone who wants to see you fail by getting complacent or getting comfortable in your own strength. The only reason you are not who you used to be is Christ. Stay in His Word and in His presence. You are made strong in your weakness (2 Corinthians 12:10).

CHAPTER 4

It Will Only Cost You Everything

Jesus never had the luxury of going to the same place every week and preaching to the same familiar faces and receiving generous offerings to cover His efforts and living expenses. In fact, searching through the Book of Matthew, at the beginning of many of the chapters, you read, "Then Jesus went. Then Jesus was led. Then Jesus traveled." The Word was always in motion. Obedience and going somewhere else always went hand in hand. In fact, almost every miracle was because Jesus traveled where He was told by the Father. Even those who brought people to Jesus for healing were because He traveled to their city. Winning the lost and complacency will never be married. Being comfortable and being called are opposite streets. Why would God Himself have to go? Why did everyone not come rushing to hear from the Messiah? Jesus, from the time He began His ministry until the time He ascended, was here as a humble servant. In fact, He went out of His way to meet the unbelieving disciples who abandoned Him. He already paid with His life and still had to go where they were! Imagine if we, the church, didn't wait for the lost to come into the building but if we went to them!

I remember the first Billy Graham crusade I witnessed on TV. I could not believe the crowds, the equipment, everything was simply amazing to see. Altar calls with tens of thousands rushing to the stage. At a young age, I was thinking, *I would love to make that kind of impact one day.* To have that influence, to lead people, what a dream to be a difference-maker. In 2018 I was planning my first crusade in the Middle East. I had no idea what I was doing. I had the message prepared, the suit picked out, and my Bible marked up. I knew thousands would be in attendance. But before I can get too far ahead, we have to step back a bit. There is planning, paying, and praying. The lights, the stage, the carpets, the chairs, the speakers, the video screen, the buses to bring the villagers in, the musicians, and the pastors' meals. Wow. I didn't realize all this was involved. My first move was to book my flight in advance. It was one thousand three hundred dollars. My visa was two hundred dollars; my private security was five hundred dollars. My vehicle transport and driver were seven hundred dollars. Visiting the slave village and feeding the families was five hundred more dollars. Preaching in the villages leading up to the crusade was two hundred dollars for each village for setup and everything else. I cannot even recall the amount to pay the local police to allow us permission. In Islamic countries, you have to do what you can do for permissions. All of these costs, and I had not even boarded the plane yet. Billy Graham did not include this part in his sermons. All I saw was the glorious entry onto the platform. I had no financial support but whatever I could sell to cover the costs. I sold my motorcycle, a car, my Rolex, and so on. How does an evangelist who nobody knows get support? Especially because I was not raised in church and lived for the world for most of my life. Maybe I could pull this one mission off to say I was able to do it. To have a lifelong testimony. Maybe when people who knew me before saw me in an Islamic country preaching Jesus, they would all pitch in and support me so I could make a go at this full-time? Either way, I was going. I remember that in one of the first missions, I gave almost every bit of money I had. In fact, I withdrew the remainder of the money that was in my account to leave for my wife and children in case something came through the account unexpectedly so that they would have plenty of money while I was gone. I had already sent all the money for everything needed while I was there, the preaching venue, the meals we were giving to the people in the village, and even my hotel stay. I just did not have any money left for me to eat for myself while I was there. It was a nine-day total mission, and I got meals on the airplane, so I figured I would fast during the mission out of necessity, and all would be good. I remember hearing stories about evangelists and missionaries going to churches and sharing their work, and churches would take up big offerings so they could go back out into the field and get back to work. The old saying is, "I will go down into the pit if you hold on to the ropes." I assumed this would be true for everyone who chose to go. Man, was I wrong in the beginning. I would come home from a mission and would have a burning testimony of how thousands were saved and miraculous signs and wonders, but nobody really wanted to hear it. I was completely puzzled. How was this not good news? Why didn't anybody want to hear what God had done? In fact, the people who used to shake my hand at church when I kept the same seat warm in each service three times a week were actually avoiding me. This was crazy! I definitely was prepared for persecution in the Middle East, but I expected a warm welcome from the ones who were supposed to be covering me in prayer. Some very close friends I had for years stopped texting, calling, and even following on Facebook. I remember posting pictures of over one thousand children in Uganda eating a meal that we provided for them because I was so happy and felt amazing. But I was getting comments from other Christians like, "Do not let your left hand know what the right hand is doing." Or, "You should help people without bragging." I remember getting angry, thinking most Christians post their new cars or new diamonds or new homes saying, "God is good," but feeding the poor and winning souls was perceived as self-promoting. I thought, *You can post things that you love that appear to be things for yourself, and I will post things that I like, such as feeding beautiful babies who have nothing and a sea of people receiving Christ for the first time.* Through this time period, I realized God did not want me to find ways to defend myself but get into His Word even more, leaving everything behind (Luke 18:22), with close friends and family abandoning me (Luke 21:16), other Christians or those I thought were Christians gossiping about me to defile my name (Matthew 7:15). And finally, as Mark 13:13 (NLT) says, "*Everyone* will hate you because you are my followers." Other versions say, "You will be hated by all men." There is a difference between going to church and following Jesus. When you go to church, your close friends and family know you are a believer, but when you follow Jesus, the whole world knows. Don't think that the weight coming down on you is a sign that you do not have the anointing to be an evangelist. The weight coming down on you is the enemy using everyone he can close to you to harm you so you will quit. The rain falls on the just and the unjust, meaning bad things happen to everyone, but the devil only attacks those who pose a threat to his kingdom. I remember preaching to a Ugandan crowd and telling them to stop blaming the devil for the rain. Rain comes down on everyone, but the devil won't mess with you if you are a closet Christian. Ephesians 6:12 (NLT) says we wrestle not against flesh and blood, but against principalities, against powers, against the rulers of the darkness of this world, against spiritual wickedness in high places. It did not take long for me to realize the price of giving your all to Jesus wasn't financial. It was much deeper. Much heavier. After establishing a family-type relationship with one of our teams in Africa, over 7,000 dollars had come up missing. All day, I stayed in bed broken. Crying and asking God, "How can someone I loved and took care of do this?" Even during COVID lockdowns, I sent money every two weeks for six of our team members to stay fed during that difficult time. I did my best to supply their needs. How could someone do this? How could I be betrayed by someone I cared about? I stopped the investigation because I didn't want to know who took the money. The money did not hurt the way the betrayal did. I realized this was a test. It was easy to love someone who loved me back, but was I able to love someone who betrayed me? I came to the realization that I could not preach a Christ that I could not be like. If you want the resurrection power, you must love Judas. Without Judas, there was no cross. Without the cross, there would be no resurrection. Without the resurrection, we have no salvation. What I am getting at is that without the betrayal, you won't have a ministry. You have to love even the ones who try to destroy you. I started realizing quickly the cost was the reason Jesus had twelve disciples and not twelve thousand. It all started making sense to me—my past, the abandonment, the separation, the black sheep. It was never a punishment for being different. It was preparation. It was training. The moment you say yes to following Jesus, the forsaking of everything else has to begin. The Christmas tree full of presents, the vacations, going to the mall on Friday nights, convertibles, and splurging for the weekend are no longer an option for someone who has died to themselves. I realized the only way to go back to normal was to go back to being normal. First Peter 2:9 (KJV) says, "But ye are a chosen generation, a royal priesthood, an holy nation, a peculiar people; that ye should shew forth the praises of him who hath called you out of darkness into his marvelous light." Peculiar people are not supposed to blend with normal ones.

There comes a point where you have to make a choice. You have to weigh out the cost of following Jesus or the cost of going back to normal. I remember when I was home from a mission for almost forty-five days. I started to feel like a lion in a cage, not doing an altar call in person for that long. My "thorn" started to get to me. It was almost a depressing state, trying to be in a normal church with three songs, a sermon, an offering, and home. Being away from the nation I was called to. They love me. They miss me and repeatedly ask if I am coming back. All while being surrounded at times in America by people who attack and criticize what Africa loves me for. It is easy to love the ones who love you, but you cannot be an evangelist only in a foreign land but also in your own town. You have to love the people who hate you. You have to extend grace to the ones who attack you. Easier said than done. They plucked the beard off Jesus, spit on Him, and pierced His side. They placed a crown of thorns on His head. He could have called down an army; instead, He called for forgiveness. He said, "Please forgive them because they do not know what they are doing." Forgiving those who have intentionally attacked me and tried to hurt me was not as easy. One day in my prayer time, God spoke and said, "Jeff, I will give you what you want. Revenge or anointing. I will not give you both, so you have to choose." I remember my eyes filling up with tears. I remembered Janet, who was called to the altar in Kenya with an inoperable terminal tumor. She was in tremendous pain and wanted to die. They could not afford another medical bill and were finished. The Lord spoke to me and said He would heal her that night in front of everyone. I remember risking the entire ministry, but I knew the voice I heard. I called her to the front and brought her on the stage. I asked her husband to accompany her. I said, "Sister, when I lay my hand on you, Jesus is going to touch you.

Not a month from now or a year from now. Not gradually, but right now in this moment." I laid my hand on her head, and tears fell from her eyes and her husband's. Two weeks later, she called our coordinator and said ever since that night, she had not had an ounce of pain or sickness. Two months after, I sent money to go get the exam. I knew she still had the doctor's reports, and deep in her mind, she doubted. She went back to the doctor, and the ultrasound proved her healing. To this day, she has been on radio programs and in churches telling what God had done for her. I could not help but think, *If I had chosen revenge, would she be alive today?* The souls that her testimony won would be on their way to hell instead. I started realizing the benefit of following Jesus was greater than the pain of being rejected by other Christians who I thought were my friends. How many people trade off their anointing for the sake of blending back in. Revivals have been terminated because people walked away from the narrow path. Matthew 7:13–14 (KJV) says, "Enter ye in at the strait gate: for wide is the gate, and broad is the way, that leadeth to destruction, and many there be which go in thereat: Because strait is the gate, and narrow is the way, which leadeth unto life, and few there be that find it." The greatest cost is not the financial means; it is giving up your life in exchange for the Great Commission. When you live your own life on your own terms, you get all your dreams. When you fulfill the Great Commission, you lose your plans, but you see the signs, the wonders, the miracles, and the flood of souls coming to the kingdom. You will witness faith unlocked. You become the hands and feet of Jesus. You will be hated by the religious, but you'll have the keys to the kingdom. Why am I investing so much time in betrayal, attacks, and criticism? Because these are the number one reason why great people with incredible callings quit. The people who seem to be against you are not your enemy. They are actually their own enemy. Going after someone who has discovered their purpose is usually just a sign that they have not discovered their own purpose. They aren't bad people; they are just lost. Having a supernatural experience with God and not knowing what to do with it can be excruciatingly painful. It is human nature. The winningest sports teams in history are also the most hated. Not because they are not good or not worthy of being liked but because they disciplined themselves to an unnatural degree simply because they decided what they wanted and knew it was possible. You get loved for your discipline and hated for your discipline. Think about it, Jesus walked on water, healed the sick, raised the dead, and raised Himself from the dead, and people still get killed today for believing in Him!

We speak so often of the New Testament revival and about wanting to see it here in the modern-day. It is one thing to study the Book of Acts, but it is another to do what they did. Acts 5:42 says, "Daily they met in the temple and from house to house, they did not cease in teaching and preaching Jesus is the Christ." We pray, "Do it again, Lord," but we must do it again too. Even slaves were preaching Christ. Revival is a mindset, not a time of year or a famous speaker coming to town. It is when we hunger and thirst for God so much on a daily basis and transmit that same passion to others, especially to the unsaved. The world will begin to ask, "What is different about that person?" "How can I get what they have?" Our lives should be so different it demands an explanation. I have realized over the years that it is the power of the Holy Spirit that brings change, not us. We have seen prostitutes become evangelists; we didn't preach prostitution; we preached the blood of Jesus. We have seen devils cast out; we didn't preach devils; we preached the blood of Jesus. We have seen murderers throw their weapons at the altar. We didn't preach against murder; we preached the blood of Jesus. We have seen women cancel their abortions, but we weren't preaching about abortions. We preached the blood of Jesus. I can go on and on. But it is the power in the blood that brings change. In today's heavy political climate, we see and hear so much of today's current events being the topic of sermons. We somehow believe that changing up the tactic will bring change. Although the condition of today's circumstances is possibly worse than the days of Sodom, and it is difficult to see and witness in our time, the way of the Spirit of God through the preaching of the Word has not gone out of style. Sometimes we need to go back to the *acts* of the early church to bring in the results we are expecting.

The most difficult thing to give up is our sin. We often declare revival and jump straight to the miracles, the fun part. It is the most fun to preach and unbelievable to witness, but true revival never has and never will begin without true repentance. In fact, James 4:8–10 says,

> Come close to God, and God will come close to you. Wash your hands, you sinners; purify your hearts, for your loyalty is divided between God and the world. Let there be tears for what you have done. Let there be sorrow and deep grief. Let there be sadness instead of laughter, and gloom instead of joy. Humble yourselves before the Lord and he will lift you up in honor.
> James 4:8–10 (NLT)

Wow, what a challenging scripture. God used a donkey, and He anointed great men who truly hated their flesh. I knew I did not want to be used because I was the only one willing; I wanted to be used because I had put grace to work and truly lost my appetite for sin. I wanted to be a conduit that wasn't full of debris but an open line for the Holy Spirit to move freely. God used me at times when I was still harboring a few things. The weight and the pressure of grieving God and sliding by another time were like carrying 500 pounds of weights in a relay race. Laying down habitual sin is not as easy as it sounds. In fact, without getting into the Word and meditating on it, it is almost impossible. In the Book of Jonah, God instructed Jonah to preach a warning message to Nineveh. Jonah did not want to do this because the people in this city were murderous and evil. Much of the way the United States of America has begun to look over the last several decades. Imagine God telling a republican to go minister to a democrat in today's society. Well, that is what God asked of Jonah. Jonah immediately rebelled. Why would God ask someone to do such a great task if He knew they would rebel? In fact, because Jonah ignored the call from God, the storm was putting the lives of the others in the boat in jeopardy. How many people are being affected because we won't put down what we want to do for what God wants? When God prepared the fish and Jonah was in the belly, he began to repent and beg God to give him another chance. He was broken over his sins and cried out to God. The Bible says that Jonah still had seaweed around his head, and he went to Nineveh immediately. Today, so many in ministry spend more time in the mirror than in their Bibles. Jonah was dirty on the outside but was cleansed on the inside. Now, do you see why God chose Jonah? God called Jonah because He saw Jonah, who Jonah was in his valley, not who he was living his best life according to his terms. Once Jonah gave up his way, God anointed him to spark a revival in a city that reached close to one million people based on the population at the time. After repentance, the journey begins.

CHAPTER 5

It's Time

Well, I know it was a rough couple of chapters. I mean, after all this, are you sure you want to go? Are you sure you are ready to sacrifice everything? As I reflect back to the beginning, I have been asked many times, "If you knew then what you know now, would you do it all over again?" The answer is "yes," and I would have started sooner. A faith that cannot be tested cannot be trusted, I have been told. Jesus viewed His life as a rescue mission. Luke 19:10 (NLT) says, "For the Son of Man came to seek and save those who are lost." His death was not a mistake; it was intentional to open the door for the salvation of whosoever would believe and call upon His name. He gave His life in exchange for ours. I have realized to be Christ-like, we must also be on a rescue mission. We must put others before ourselves. Jesus came to this earth in the form of a man for the sole purpose of saving mankind. This is not just for us to know; it is for us to carry and tell. Many times I wanted to give up and quit. Each time I went anyway, the move of God was even more unbelievable than the last time. Reflecting back on my very first crusade, from witnessing God raise a dead baby to seeing a tumor disappear, to future crusades where we witnessed the lame walking, lepers being healed, witch doctors surrendering to Christ, and so on, the revelation God has revealed and the testimonies I have witnessed far surpass any fire I have had to go through to get to those testimonies. One of the final crusades of 2021 was in Migori county in Kenya, as I mentioned in an earlier chapter. We had hired a famous African musician to bring the crowds. Our name was well known in major cities, but in the smaller unreached areas, we had to get creative to bring in the crowds. When the musician was finishing on the first night, about one hundred of the several thousand people started to leave. Before they called me to the platform, one of the pastors tried to convince them all to stay. I was laughing to myself. When I approached the pulpit, I recall telling the crowd that I was not worried about the ones who had left because I was going to preach so loud that they would hear me in their homes. The first two nights of the crusade, like all of them, over 85 percent of the crowd stood for salvation. Thousands. But the final night, something was different. God spoke to me and said, "Tonight is a John Chapter 4 night." God said, "You came here for one person." God sent me 10,000 miles to meet with one person. So I asked each person to stay seated at that altar call. In Genesis 12, Abraham was called to the mission field. He had to leave everything. In Genesis Chapter 22, Abraham was bringing his son Isaac to the mountain top for a sacrifice to prove God's gift was not greater than God Himself. Isaac saw how crazily committed his father was. In Genesis 26, Isaac was digging wells, and every time he would strike water, the enemy would come to fill in the well and take claim to it. Because Isaac had a champion for a father who had an obedience that at the time could not be matched, he kept digging another well. Isaac never gave up because his father never gave up. In John Chapter 4, Jesus was exhausted from a long journey through Samaria, which was way out of the way from His destination (very similar to Migori county, when our main crusade was ten hours north in Nairobi). Jesus rested at a well. At this well was one of the most significant meetings in the New Testament. An undeserving sinful woman was transformed that day into one of the first evangelists to win her home city. What was interesting was that this well that proposed the meeting spot was a well that was owned by Jacob. Jacob, who was the son of Isaac, who never stopped digging wells during hard times, and who was the grandson of Abraham, who left everything behind to do what God said. From the very beginning of Abraham's journey, God had this Samaritan woman in mind. Abraham didn't know, but he went anyway. God told me there was a woman there who He sent me to lay hands on and introduce her to Jesus. God also told me (which all is documented) that night would be this woman's only opportunity to go. Many have hundreds of chances, but that night was her only chance to receive Jesus. Then out of nowhere, a woman came carrying another woman to the altar. She could barely stand on her own. Her friend spoke and said, "My friend's name is Zainab. She has been hearing you preach each night from her living room but could not have the strength to get here. I felt led to bring her. She has had a terrible sickness for over a month now and needs prayer." I lowered the microphone and said, "Honey, I am going to lay my hand on you, and Jesus is going to move, starting right now." Before I could touch her, she fell to the ground. She started screaming and rolling on the ground. The spirits in her started to manifest. The power of the Holy Ghost was too strong for these demons to hide. After approximately twelve minutes, she was free. They helped her to her feet, and we led her to Christ.

I told her that her testimony and how God had chosen her and sent me thousands of miles to meet her would be told all over, and millions would come to Jesus because of what God had just done for her. I still did not know why God told me this would be her only chance, but we were rejoicing. It was one week from that time, and the call came in, "Evangelist Jeff, Zainab has gone to be with Jesus." I immediately started to cry. It all made sense. I thought she was going to share her testimony everywhere, but we were the ones with the platform to tell millions and win millions. God knew her time was up, so He moved heaven and earth for one young girl named Zainab to be saved before she went home. Most of it made sense to me, but in John 4, the woman at the well won her city, so it seemed something was missing. I was then asked to preach her funeral over video from the United States. I was honored. Right before the altar call, I remember saying, "At this moment, Zainab is telling all the angels, 'Everyone, wait just a moment. Hold the harp and the piano. Don't play anything yet. Because in two minutes, I am about to see the fruit of my one week of being born again on that earth. I am about to see my purpose.'" So all the angels just sat in silence. The altar call was given. Fifty-seven people out of the crowd came forward for salvation, and heaven erupted. Zainab grabbed an instrument she had never played on earth and led all the angels in heaven in the most beautiful song of praise and celebration. The whole thing made sense. I witnessed John Chapter 4 come to life all over again. I cannot always start quoting the Bible in the short amount of time I go to each department store and gas station, but I can quote what God had done for one woman who everyone else had written off. To this day, Impact Nations Global has adopted Kennedy, her seven-year-old son. He started school for the first time and got a birth certificate made up because he never even had one before. Kennedy has a shot at a great future. He does not remember his mother as a demon-possessed bartender. He remembers his mother as the evangelist who won fifty-seven souls while in paradise! Anything of great value comes with a high price tag. Miracles are rare because anointing is rare. Anointing is rare because obedience is rare. Obedience is rare because faith is dormant. The word "faith" in the Western world is saying that God will do it. But the word "faith" in Hebrew is an action-oriented word meaning "support" or "one who supports God." This biblical definition is also referenced in Exodus 17:12. It changes everything by shifting the meaning to its original context. The Superbowl is not won on Superbowl Sunday; it is won in every practice leading up to the game. If you practice like you are going to win, you train harder, work harder, stay later, and do one more lap than is required. The reward of discipline is always greater than the inconvenience. To whom much is given, much is required. If you live in the most blessed country on the planet with the greatest opportunities in the world, there is an obligation to do more, be more, and become more. How many times we go to church is not as relevant as how many times we become the church. Evangelist, your job is to build relationships with pastors. They carry a different anointing than you. You start the fire; they fan the flames. We need one another. The majority of churches are going backward because there are no new sheep. Revelation chapters 2 and 3 both mention going back to how you were when you were first saved, to the work you did at first. There is something special about that fresh fire. It is better to not know everything but to act on the little you do know than to continue to gain knowledge but never apply it. Brand new people take action. If there are no new people, it is a weekly meeting of complacency and comfort, which offers no threat to a never-sleeping enemy. It is time to rise up. We have heard the Word of God; we must now become doers of the Word. Winning souls and not plugging them in is extremely dangerous. We are all the church, and all have a different anointing. We need each other.

According to *Bible.org*, 95 percent of all Christians have never won a soul to Christ. Eighty percent of all Christians do not consistently witness for Christ. Less than 2 percent are involved in the ministry of evangelism. Seventy-one percent do not give toward the financing of the Great Commission. When people come into the building, the money comes in; when people go out of the building, so does the money. For some, every time they get a dollar, they get a soul; for others, every time they get a soul, they get a dollar. If God has called you, He will make a way. Do not wait for the funding to come. It costs nothing to tell someone about Jesus. Once you do what you can with what you have, God will increase so that you can go further. His Word is like a lamp unto your feet and a light unto your path. The thing about a lamp is that you cannot see the entire path, just your next step. Take one step at a time. With each step, the light will get brighter. When you can be trusted with the little you have, you'll be able to be trusted with more. On my first trip to Nairobi, Kenya, I traveled

10,000 miles, and I preached to twenty people. I wanted to be disappointed. In fact, I asked God why He sent me there. It did not make sense. I thought I would have a huge crowd. I remember preaching so hard to those twenty people despite my disappointment. Seventeen of the twenty gave their heart to Christ. I encouraged them to bring more the next night. By the final night, there were sixty people. A man in a wheelchair got up and walked right out of the church, and the piano player had a deep-rooted demon that came out that night. Despite the small number of people, there was a move of the Holy Ghost. I realized that I would no longer be focused on the size of the crowd but be focused on my job. One year later, in Kenya, there was a one hundred and fifty motorcycle motorcade escorting us in with police commandos bringing us to a crowd of thousands of people who wanted to witness what happened in that church with the twenty people! I was mocked and ridiculed for traveling so far for twenty but never once thought about quitting. Why? Because I realized that while people who never leave the pew were concerned about the crowd, they didn't even care that the Holy Spirit showed up. I'd rather preach to five people in the presence of the Lord than 500,000 people using my own intellect and talent.

EVANGELISM: THE PROCESS

Nairobi, Kenya, November 2021. Standing on the platform, looking out to a sea of beautiful African people hungry and waiting on a move from God.

On the first night of the crusade, almost 90 percent of the crowd received Christ. But something felt heavy. I remembered when Elijah had the showdown on Mount Carmel with Ahab and 450 other prophets. Elijah told them he would stand there and wait for Baal to send fire from heaven, and if their god did not perform, he would gladly show them how the God of heaven and earth would surely respond. Elijah began to mock their belief in a false god. It was a rather funny situation because God showed up and showed out to the point where the people who put their belief in Baal started cutting themselves with their knives. I felt a demonic presence of witchcraft that night—many in that crowd had their faith in witchcraft and witch doctors. I grabbed the microphone, and the final call was an invitation. An invitation for every demon, every witch, and every witch doctor to come with everything they had on the following night. I committed to them that Jesus would be there and every one of them would be delivered and filled with real power. The team got into our transport vehicle and laughed and said, "Man, you just invited every witch and mocked their false god." The next day I kept mostly to myself, leading to the final night of the crusade. I knew what was coming. At the altar call, we had to remove the ropes to let everyone get close to the stage. My wife laid hands on one woman, and the showdown began.

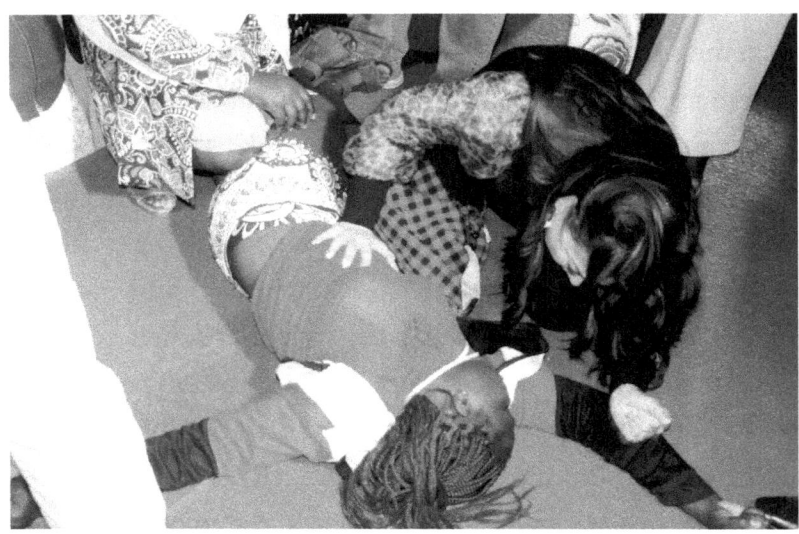

People began pushing and fighting to get to the altar. That woman and the spirit in her began to manifest. At the same time, another and another. I called all the men on the team, every usher, every pastor, and my wife to work. One after another. Bodies were everywhere. The pastors grabbed me and said, "This demon said it is the leader, and it wants you." I rushed over. She said, "We came to kill you. We brought knives in the crowd, and we are going to kill her when we are done," referring to the vessel the demon was occupying. She made a stabbing motion towards her stomach, just like the 450 prophets who were worshipping Baal. She was yelling, "Who are you?" but refused to look at me. I said, "Look at me," and she said that she could not because it hurt her eyes. I believe the fire God sent from heaven through the Holy Spirit was too much. She kept repeating, "We are going to kill her." When the final spirit left her body, I sat her up to ask how she was, and she could not speak any English. Not one word. The remainder of the conversation with her had to be translated. I looked around, and bodies were still twisting everywhere, so I went from person to person, casting out demon after demon, just like everyone on the team. It was nothing like I had ever seen. After over four hours of casting out demons, I had not even realized it, but most of the crowd was still there watching what the Lord had done. After the last person was delivered, we barely made it to our vehicle under our own strength. Just like on Mount Carmel, the Lord sent His fire down in Nairobi, Kenya. It was total silence in the car. Nobody could talk after what had just happened. Everyone felt so weak; they were fighting sickness, exhaustion, and so many other things. Many did not sleep for days after what they witnessed. Every single demon, every witch, and every witch doctor came to fight, and everyone left delivered. Hundreds of demons were cast out. To this day, that area in Nairobi is begging for another crusade. Prostitutes who were delivered brought ten more prostitutes the next week to church. One of the prostitutes came to the altar, got delivered, and her son, who had not walked in months, began to walk. She has not missed a church service since that night.

EVANGELISM: THE PROCESS

The most recent crusade in the Middle East, at the Pakistan and Afghanistan border, was the most incredible crowd I had seen before me.

As I was exiting our transport vehicle with the Secret Service and the Pakistan government security escort, I was guided up to the platform, where I was welcomed by a crowd of just under four hundred thousand people, according to the event coordinators. After a twenty-minute sermon, the altar call was given. When I asked for a public confession of Christ in front of the Taliban and many other groups, over three hundred thousand hands went in the air. I placed my face in my hands and just wept for a moment before I could even pray with all who made a decision that night. I am telling you right now that the revelation, the anointing, and the power of

God are the reward waiting for you here on this earth. It is reserved for you. Not for the average, the lukewarm, or the comfortable but the obedient. Every attack, every struggle, every problem becomes a pebble compared to the magnitude of what you will see and experience. Everything you read in God's Word will come to life before your eyes. Most will only get to hear it in your testimony, but God will reveal it to you! Do not give up. Do not surrender your permanent reward for the temporary relief that comes with turning back. Pray for your enemies, love people, and walk in the will of God. Preach Jesus while adopting His character. The further you go, the more He will show you. In fact, many of the people who hurt me in the beginning have called and asked for forgiveness. God will turn your enemies into allies if you stay the course. The glory belongs to Jesus. One day the crown that is placed upon your head, you will be able to remove and place at the feet of the one who bled and died for you and me. You will hear one day, "Well done, My good and faithful servant." You have fought the good fight, you have finished your course, and you have remained faithful. There is a crown laid up for you of righteousness, which the Lord, the righteous Judge, shall give you on the day of His return. That price is not only for you but for all who eagerly look forward to His appearing (2 Timothy 4:7–8). Many believe that full-time ministry is when you get paid enough to preach that you do not have to go to work for money. But in reality, full-time ministry is when you wake up with a burning desire to serve our Lord Jesus by fulfilling His commands. To love one another and to tell someone about Him. I keep a diary every day to track how many souls our team has led to Jesus. Each and every day. I have always been a goal-oriented person. I believe that if you aim at nothing, you will hit the target of nothing every time. Churches make giving goals, membership goals, and many other targets each and every week. As an evangelist, my heart is to advance each day. If we do not get closer to the target each day, then we are getting further away. There is no staying the same. We are either growing or dying. It is not possible to know Jesus and love people but avoid telling of His goodness and mercy. Oftentimes the Sunday service is a sermon based on a crowd of people who know and understand some of the Word. But brand new believers are somewhat lost during most sermons. This is where the pews must come alive. Discipleship is key. Modern Christianity says, "Go ye therefore and find new members," but the scripture still says, "Make disciples." Discipleship comes with a cost. It is not the pastor's responsibility to disciple every individual who walks in the door. This is where the pews need to take action. A member of a church who has attended service after service and has heard sermon after sermon should be discipling someone else at any given time. Costless Christianity has led to a drought of miracles in many first-world countries. Starting from the beginning with a brand new believer will strengthen your foundation in the process. The teacher often learns more than the student. If Jesus was always in motion while He walked this earth, and the disciples were always in motion, it only makes sense that we should be too.

I remember after a prayer meeting, we were preparing to leave the home we were meeting in. I went downstairs to find our daughter. I looked everywhere but could not find her. I went to take one last look after going back upstairs to see if she had come up. I finally found her in a corner alone, playing on her tablet. I thought it was odd to be that far isolated and alone when there were other kids nearby. So I bent down and asked her if everything was okay and why she was sitting in the corner. She said, "I wanted to plug my tablet in so it didn't die." I looked at her tablet, and it was fully charged. It sort of reminded me of the days when home phones had a long cord, and you could only talk in that one room. It was like being stuck. I couldn't imagine today if people couldn't communicate but in one place again. God instantly spoke to me, saying that this is the picture of the church. You have people fully charged but not leaving the church. The only time we communicate or praise is near the outlet. Mobile phones were meant to be mobile. To leave the charging stations and return when they are almost empty of charge. I watch people charge their devices while they are almost fully charged all the time. You have to leave the church building to win the world. They are not coming in; you have to go out. Nobody ever charges a phone or tablet with no intention of using it. So why would we get filled with the Word and more knowledge and never use it? To whom much is given, much is required. When you go back to church, go back empty. Pour out what you have each week. The church building isn't where you work; it is the report card for the work you did in the world. It is important that this generation paves the way for the next generation. Build something bigger than our own name. Let the name of Jesus be the way. We have to fight today with everything we have so that the road is paved. The generation coming up can step up to the pulpit that we had to spend so much time building. The fruit of your obedience can reach from generation to generation. You will never see the fruits here on earth because they will grow long after you're gone. The reward that awaits you in the next life will reveal the depth of your sacrifice in this life. It will all be worth it. Who that is for you is greater than who that is against you. Be the light of the world, a city on a hill that cannot be ignored. Second Peter 1:10 (NLT) says, "So, dear brothers and sisters, work hard to prove that you really are among those

God has called and chosen. Do these things, and you will never fall away." Idle time is not for true believers. God has given you a purpose and a plan. Stay true to the calling, and God will keep you from falling. Let the whole world know, starting in Jerusalem (local), Judea (your state), Samaria (your country), and all the ends of the earth, that Jesus Christ is alive in you, and together we will plunder hell to populate heaven, as the late Reinhard Bonnke used to say.

CPSIA information can be obtained
at www.ICGtesting.com
Printed in the USA
JSHW050253090922
30254JS00006B/164